W9-BNI-215

TRANSFIGURATIONS
PLACES OF PRAYER

Richard England
Linda Schubert

Foreword
Myriam England

Introduction
Richard Demarco

Afterword
Robert Faricy S.J.

Richard England
Linda Schubert

TRANSFIGURATIONS
Places of Prayer

Cover Photo
Peter Bartolo Parnis

Photography
Joseph Cassar
Anthony Cassar Desain
Richard England
Joseph A. Vella

All projects and drawings
Richard England

Richard England
Fax: (356) 334263
e-mail: myriam@vol.net.mt

Linda Schubert
P.O. Box 4034
Santa Clara CA 95056
U.S.A.
e-mail: linda@linda-schubert.com
www.linda-schubert.com

First edition April 2000

Publishing Coordinators
Antonio Carbone
Pasquale Ciliento

Graphic Design
Maria Teresa Quinto

Printing
Finiguerra Arti Grafiche
Lavello

ISBN 88-87202-06-0

CONTENTS

STATEMENT OF INTENT

Architecture besides providing stability and emotion must above all provide a practical solution to the problem which generated it. Therefore it may be termed a servient art. In the creation of sacred spaces, the architect is faced with perhaps the most arduous of tasks; how can a physical space respond to what remains basically a spiritual need ? The object of this publication is to put Richard England's prayer arenas to this test, having Linda Schubert in her capacity as a woman of prayer, not only experiencing these spaces and documenting her reactions but also providing to the reader her personal prayers inspired in her moments of silence within these *loci*.

The bringing together of the maker's intentions and the users' reactions as pointed out in the foreword by Myriam England, provides a fascinating amalgamation of design purpose and actual function, bearing in mind that the ultimate aim of a sacred space is to provide a threshold-platform to enable mankind to make contact with the Creator.

FOREWORD

I have known Linda Schubert for six years. Prior to our meeting, I was given her best selling publication *Miracle Hour* when it first appeared in 1991. It was a book which was to have a tremendous impact on my life; for it provided me, first of all with a quest and thirst for a knowledge of the Holy Scriptures, and also initiated in me a search for a deeper level of quiet time and prayer. So influenced was I by its messages that I found myself endlessly distributing copies to friends and acquaintances. I have no doubt that the book and its author were endorsed with a special anointing and I know that the many people who have had access to the book have eventually come to experience a very personal relationship with the Lord.

Three years after I had been introduced to the publication, I had the privilege of attending one of Linda Schubert's healing sessions in London. I immediately felt that I was being inspired and directed to invite her to my native island of Malta for teaching and healing sessions. I therefore ventured to introduce myself and actually extend the invitation. The meeting was to be the beginning of a very close and special friendship which keeps growing and developing to this very day. I have also been blessed, in my capacity as Co-ordinator of the Malta Chapter of Magnificat, to invite Linda to be our guest speaker on a number of occasions. These visits to my island plus many others have endeared her to all the members of my family and she is now very much an essential part of us.

I have an even closer relationship with the other author of this book. Ever since I met Richard, my husband, even prior to our marriage, his life has been dedicated to architecture and design, with special interest in the theories involved in the making of sacred spaces. I well remember, many years back, when he was still a student in the studio of Gio Ponti in Milan, that he had sent me sketches of his initial ideas for the church at Manikata in Malta. Twelve years in the making, this building was to become an icon of contemporary Christian church design, pre-empting many of the norms outlined in Vatican II. Over the years, although Richard has been involved with many important secular projects both in Malta and in other countries, his main concern has remained focussed on the architectural and theological aspects of the making of sacred spaces. Of late he has further focussed this interest on the concept of the private chapel space in the home.

Bearing in mind Richard's commitment to the theme and my special relationship with Linda, the idea of this publication was born. At a moment of prayer in our family home chapel I experienced a strong prompting that Linda and Richard should come together to produce a book. Richard's approach to a methodology of design of sacred spaces and his conviction that faith is the most essential of all the architect's creative tools in this aspect of work, and Linda as a woman of deep prayer experiencing these spaces and documenting her personal reaction to these chapels, would make a unique and particular combination. I could see the publication with its emphasis on domestic private prayer spaces and their *transfiguration* into sacred spaces, and Linda's relationship to them, providing a fascinating amalgamation documenting both the maker's and the user's intentions and reactions. I envisaged that this book, about the making of arenas conceived as springboards to reach the Lord, would itself also reach out to the many sensitive human hearts which are searching to fill their emptiness. It was St Augustine who said, *"the soul will only find rest when it rests in Him."*

Following this prompting, with a sense of exuberance I faxed Linda and also spoke to Richard about the project. Both were more than enthusiastic and they worked together on the idea for many months. The book, I am sure, will be particularly pertinent not only to artists and architects, but also to all who are searching for spiritual solace and meaning in their lives.

I augur that all who leaf through this book be blessed, not only through the visual beauty of Richard's spaces and the depth and sincerity of Linda's prayers inspired within their walls, but most of all by the obvious love of the Lord manifest in its pages. Above all I augur that it will serve as a working tool for its readers to develop and experience a very unique and personal relationship with God, our Father.

"God is love. Whoever lives in God lives in love and God lives in Him." (1 John 4:16)

Myriam England

INTRODUCTION

"Sacred" is not a word used by most architects nowadays. However, in the case of Richard England, Malta's internationally renowned architect, it is a word he uses naturally and frequently. Perhaps this is because, at heart, he is that rare bird in the architectural profession world-wide, who wishes to fly higher than most architects, into the rarified atmosphere in which poets and artists aspire to the eternal verities particularly those who respect the spiritual dimension which Joseph Beuys, arguably the 20th Century successor to Leonardo Da Vinci, described as *"element three"*. Where is element three ? This was the question Beuys asked of himself as an artist-scientist.

Richard England asks the same question in relation not only to his own work, but in his enquiries into the history of architecture. He asks simply: *"Where is the sacred ?"* To help answer that question he has given himself the task, often self-appointed, of focusing upon the building of spaces for prayer and meditation. Those which he has built in Malta are recognizably chapels or churches, and all have been tried and tested by Linda Schubert who has dedicated herself to a life of prayer and searching for the experience of her Lord and Saviour, Jesus Christ. I accompanied her on her first journey into Richard England's choice of seven sacred spaces which for him can be regarded as prayer made visible. They are the concretisation of the sacred. Richard England led the one-day expedition, accompanied by his wife Myriam, who regards Linda Schubert as a close friend and a source of inspiration in her own personal search for a spiritual life. The expedition was conducted in the spirit of a pilgrimage by the immediate response of Linda Schubert to each prayerful space she entered. She found herself inspired to pray.

The first was the chapel Richard England made for himself and family at the house in St Julians, bequeathed to him by his father as a distinguished architect. In a room close to the main door there was what Richard England calls the "Home Chapel". It is a small domestic space dominated by the image of a cross set in a recess. It could be, in fine art terms, considered as a piece of contemporary sculpture and it serves to bridge the gap between the contemporary artist and that of the priest and pilgrim.

The second point on the pilgrimage was the M.U.S.E.U.M. Chapel in Blata l-Bajda. It is a dark, enclosed, windowless space again dominated by a cross, with the addition of a pyramidial sculpture enclosed within a black metal grill. Behind the cross there is a red wall. Artificial lighting is so positioned that the shadows of the grill are projected upon the walls and ceiling. The ceiling consists of a number of planes, designed to accept lovingly the shadows of the grill.

On the third stage we encountered for the first time, the evidence of an altar in Richard England's concept of a sacred space and behind it, is a large-scale crucifix rather than a bare cross. This chapel, known as the Meditation Chapel of the M.U.S.E.U.M. at Naxxar brought Linda Schubert to tears of gratitude for the way in which it inspired her to pray. Malta stone is used in the form of free standing walls and the ceiling is vaulted. Next to the altar is a circular stone table which acts as a lectern for the reading of the Word of God. There is also a stone chair.

The next experience of a Richard England sacred space was again on a small scale in the shape of the tiny room which functions as the meditation chapel in the Franciscan House at Burmarrad. Again there is no altar and again the cross is bare. The cross stands as an integral part of a six-stepped sculpture form, painted white. The ceiling is curved and so too are the two walls, one painted purple and the other light blue. They help focus attention on the cross. The carpeted floor is at an angle to give the impression that the whole room is tilting.

The next stage of the pilgrimage took us on the road to a converted Maltese farmhouse in which dwells Sandrina Darmanin, the daughter of Richard and Myriam England. It is called Sandrina's Chapel and acts as a family chapel for her and her husband, her three sons and daughter. The floor is made of paved local stone surrounded by stone chippings. The walls are of concrete to make it uncompromisingly modern. There is a square form slab of stone defining the altar. This is positioned to the extreme left of centre. There is a stone screen as a background. On the opposite side to the altar, beside the right hand side wall, is a small crucifix, again without the physical form of Christ's body, emphasizing the Resurrection.

The largest and most joyful chapel space is that of "The Chapel of Light" at Dar il-Hanin Samaritan. This caused Linda again to cry tears of gratitude as she recognised what she called "the light of Christ". The exterior is a hymn of praise to the Maltese baroque - but simplified. The interior is dominated by the crucified form of Christ suspended in front of a cross positioned on a blue square slab. The figure is thus released from the cross. The altar is carved from a monolithic piece of Malta stone. The chapel is lit by innumerable small square windows recessed in white painted concrete walls. Each glass window is thick and opaque and forms an exhibitionist abstract painting free flowing with blue and white images. The windows are so arranged that they reproduce a shelf-like source of light.

From the road to Sandrina's chapel, dominating the village of Manikata set on the upper slopes of a terraced valley is the parish church of St Joseph. This church is Richard England's response to Le Corbusier's Chapel of Ronchamp. It is the work of a youthful England. It was this church which attracted the attention in the late sixties of both Sir Basil Spence and Victor Pasmore who both decided to use Richard England as their architect. Manikata's exterior is made of concrete to achieve the curvilinear sculptural forms. The surface is painted a warm brown: the colour of the fields around the village. There are four apertures in the form of doors or windows. The interior contains the church sculpture of the old parish church of Manikata: fitting surprisingly well into the resolute modernity of the whole building.

Richard England designed the Papal Pavilions for the Pope's visit to Malta in 1990. These transformed large public spaces in Floriana to prove without deceit his capacity to make a large-scale outdoor sacred space with a mixture of Malta stone and painted concrete. The Papal throne surmounted an impressive flight of steps. Placed behind this focal point was a large cross. Sky blue, pink, light purple were the pastel colours used on the defining walls in harmony with the natural Malta stone.

The most recent sacred space which Richard England had to consider was the Church of St Francis of Assisi at Qawra. This large scale opus is located in a distinctly urban area. Richard England has somehow managed to build a sacred building which can compete with the large scale apartments and hotels which have proliferated the surrounding area in recent years. Behind the church's main altar designed to conform with the new liturgy and Vatican Two, there is a large sculpture of the crucified Christ. It suggests He is freeing Himself from the restricted symbol of the Cross which is behind Him on a flat square panel. The altar is set on the first level of a flight of steps so that the congregation has a clear view of the Sanctum-Sanctorum area around the main altar. Malta stone, painted concrete and marble constitute the stuff and substance of this cathedral-like building. The roof lies heavenwards high above the heads of the congregation. This sacred space above all the others, embodies the evidence required to comprehend what Richard England means by sacred architecture. It is his response to all the sacred spaces he has taken the trouble to experience for himself over the past forty years from the Megalithic Temples of his beloved Malta leading to Malta's baroque churches and chapels, and to places well known and unknown, from chapels to obscure shrines and chapels all over Europe and in the wider world. He is the personification of the European architect fully prepared to use the energy of the Christo-Judaic dynamic in an age sorely in need of the sacred space made manifest in modern architecture.

Richard Demarco

TRANSFIGURATIONS

As a close friend of Richard England's wife, Myriam, I have had the privilege of making many visits to their home in Malta. On my first trip, I was given a tour of Richard's chapels. Although I have visited many chapels in countless countries, none have moved me as profoundly as these. My personal reactions to the private prayer places of Richard England are recorded in a later chapter.

This joint venture with Richard is exciting, because it provides such a unique blend. We come from different worlds, yet in his chapels I often feel very much at home. Certain environments, like perfect sunsets and Richard's chapels, can literally draw people into God's presence. Prayer doesn't come easily, but it is the most worthwhile activity we can ever engage in. That is why I spend my life praying, writing and conducting prayer seminars.

There is a growing urgency in people around the world to contact the sacred. People experiment with all manner of things to connect with the divine. They run after gurus, try mind altering drugs and create their own gods, seeking something higher than themselves. Yet God is yearning for them to find a quiet place, and turn to Him. He is just waiting for people to set aside the heaped-up activities and noisy distractions long enough to hear His voice.

My own approach to *Transfigurations* is through the doorway of a deep Christian faith, expressed through the Catholic tradition. While Richard's chapels invite reflection on the cross of Jesus, the symbol of God's love for us, our desire is for people of all faiths to be welcomed, awakened and inspired by the chapels and writings of Richard England, and through my simple words of hope and prayer. To welcome people of all faiths we will speak of "God" or "Lord", except at those times we are addressing a specifically Christian form of prayer, where we might mention Jesus. We offer this book with great love.

What is prayer ? Prayer is homecoming. It begins when we lift our heart and mind to God in the sanctuary of our spirit. The interaction may be verbal or silent, structured or free form and involves an exchange of communication that can become intimate communion. The important thing is that we begin talking to God in earnest, and begin listening as He speaks to us.

Christian prayer is communion with God as loving Father through union with Jesus Christ and by the action of the Holy Spirit. Every ritual of Christian prayer is meant to guide the person through the form to the person of Jesus. Christian denominations may vary, but all agree upon salvation through the cross of Jesus Christ.

For me, prayer is honest, open heart-to-heart communion with a God who loves me and cares for me like a father. The relationship with God in prayer has grown from seeking my own way, to participating in His will being accomplished. One evening I began my prayer time with "Lord I just want to love You". Three hours later I ended the prayer time, knowing I had contacted God.

My spirit yearns for both public and private prayer. With a deeply contemplative nature, I love solitary prayer, yet I also long for times of fervent, even noisy public worship. Christians learn that Jesus prayed in various locations, public and private: in the desert, in the garden, on the mountains, in the synagogue, in the upper room and on the cross. We are exhorted to "pray continually" but learn that unless we set aside a time of solitude and silence each day, it is very difficult or nearly impossible to "pray constantly". One of the values of solitary prayer is that we tend to become more open with God. There is no one watching us but God, and without people around, we are more genuine.

Private prayer is meant to be as individual as the person, and public prayer can be a structured ritual or free form, or a combination. Personal prayer time can supply nourishment for greater participation in public prayer. Public prayer can provide fuel for a deeper experience of private prayer. Each nurtures the other, as one leg follows another. Once I heard about a man so deeply moved by Gregorian chant in a medieval cathedral that he was overcome by the power of God, and was drawn into a whole new life of individual prayer. A nun attending one of my Christian conferences in Canada was so enraptured by the power of the praise music in the large assembly that she experienced a release of singing in what is described as the language of the Spirit. The transforming moment increased the fruitfulness of her private prayer.

Linda Schubert

IN SEARCH OF SACRED SPACES

INTRODUCTION

"The greatest challenge for an architect remains the Church."

These words, written by Antonio Gaudi, the designer of perhaps the most exuberant and ebullient religious structure of the 20th Century, The Sagrada Familia in Barcelona, Spain emphasize the immense challenge which an architect faces in the design of a church as a place of gathering and prayer.

Religious architecture, manifesting man's attempt to create sacred spaces, from pre-history through history, has always been expressed as a manifestation in built-form of his understanding of the Divine at that particular moment in time. Current beliefs and theology have inevitably always formed the basis of man's attempt to provide spaces of worship (at times conceived as the actual residences of the Divinity) in which he could pay homage and pray.

ORIGINS

"Know ye that ye are the temple of God, and that the spirit of God dwelleth in you." (St. Paul)

Referring to the Holy Book, and in particular to the chapters of Genesis, we find that in the creation of Eden, the paradisiacal habitat planned for man by his Creator; God, in His supreme majesty and infinite wisdom, did not build a <u>house</u> for man, but a <u>garden.</u> Man, on the other hand, yielding perhaps to the human temptations of arrogance and pride, has for most of his time of existence on this planet, built <u>houses</u> for his God or gods. The following verses of the same Book continue to provide us with relative information re the origins of the architectural profession. Here we come across the first reference to man in his activity as a builder. In Chapter 4 verse 17, it is recounted that Cain, after the murder of his brother Abel, and after the Lord had banished him from his enclave of fertile fields, moved to the land of Nod where he founded and built a city which he named Enoch. Not perhaps the best ancestral pedigree for the architectural profession. However Cain, with his concept of community and settlement must eventually be acknowledged as the founder of civilization. Five generations later his descendents were already playing musical instruments, forging metal, and weaving; all clear signs of a civilized and organized pattern of life.

A more rewarding version of the origin of the architect is given in a story recounted by the Italian architect-designer Gio Ponti. In his book "Amate l'Architettura", the text refers to the first Age of Creation and tells the following tale. As God in His majesty watched and enjoyed the evolution and development of His newly created Universe, He frequently sent angels down to earth to acquaint them with the marvels of His creations. Some of the more inquisitive of these winged creatures re-entered the Gates of Paradise with objects and artifacts gathered from Earth, which they then showed Him: a rose, a tool, wine and various other extraordinary things. God would simply state that these did not in any way surprise Him as, after all, they were well known to Him as they were but His own creations. The tool was made of iron, a material which He had created in the first place and the wine was a product made from grapes which He had originated and then planted in the Garden. However, one day, a number of angels (the even more inquisitive ones) appeared with examples of paintings, poems, musical scores, a piece of sculpture and also, (presumably after much combined angelic effort) the manifestation of an architectural project in terms of a completed building. With all these objects at His feet, God, seeing that these were not His creations, decided it was time to call the angels to a meeting to furnish an explanation and pronounce a definitive Divine definition of art. *'Art, gentlemen angels, is the miracle of man. It is something created by man, and it is his most beautiful and greatest achievement. It is man's Divine achievement, in which, and in which alone, he is like Me. He is a Creator.'*

Man created by his Creator becomes in his own right the creator. As Gio Ponti continues to say this is *"a real miracle, performed by those who cannot perform miracles!"* The narrative of this story, in contrast to the Cain version, provides a more decorous and acceptable version of the origin of the architectural and building profession.

TEMPLES IN TIME

"A manifestation of the Sacred is always a revelation of Being." (Mircea Eliade)

Ever since man's displacement from his first dwelling, the man-made temple through time becomes the metaphor of the desire to return to the Edenic paradisiacal state of innocence. A brief run-through man's attempts in time to provide spaces of worship manifests not only his constant preoccupation with the supremacy of his God or gods, but also his propensity to fashion these gathering spaces to suit the particular theologies of the different periods. Ever since the earliest moments of his existence on this planet, man has felt that in relation to the totality of the cosmos, he plays but a small part. In order to come to terms with these forces beyond recognition, he has directed prayer and made offerings to his gods or pantheon of gods depending on his creed and belief of the moment. At all times there is an attempt to link the limited voices of humanity to the open oracles of the gods. It is true to say that the greatest architectural works of all civilizations have been accomplished in religious or allied buildings of worship reflecting man's respect and fear of the powers of the Divine. It seems that the more difficult survival was, the greater the effort man would devote to placate his gods. Always, in this context, man, in his buildings, attempts to outlast and defy, if not defeat, time. Religious buildings, in the concept of extending temporality, contrast strongly with man's humility and resigned admission to a temporal existence when building for himself. In building for the Divine, man attempts to leave a permanent sign to reach beyond his own limited time as if to fix in no-time the co-ordinates of a spatio-temporal equation mapping his path and existence on this planet.

Malta's own Neolithic temples, dating back some 5000 years, demonstrate a community's deep concern for successful harvest crops and consequent survival by practising a fertility cult related to a Divinity of the Earth. These earth-focussed, sky-oriented container spaces may be read as an almost direct translation in built-form of the body of the goddess. Amorphous and orbicular in format, these "temples" utilized a highly sophisticated building technology to evoke man's understanding of his dependency on the earth and the movement of heavenly bodies. The temple culture of the Maltese Islands, expressed in giant megaliths, is a manifestation of a peoples' awe, trepidation and respect of the forces and powers of nature and its laws.

As in the temples of ancient Greece, the Maltese examples were conceived as specific loci built by man for the gods to dwell in, distinctively inaccessible to the community of believers. Many of the Divine dwelling places, as recounted in ancient myths and indeed in the Holy Book itself, had their dimensions laid out and specified by the very gods themselves. In the later Christian tradition the concept of the sacred space functioning as the house of God is less evident. The solutions in Christianity have instead leaned more towards the concept of a gathering space for worshippers to congregate in, adhering perhaps to the prophet Isaiah's words that *"God does not dwell in houses built by man"*. In the soaring perpendicular spaces of the mid-Second Millennium Nordic Cathedrals the floating lattices of the Gothic vaulted ceilings crystallize man's belief at the time in a God of wrath and power. The splendour of the German and Italian Baroque manifested in almost operatic opulence focusses on an extravaganza of undulating surfaces to emphasize the supreme majesty and glory of the Divine Creator. In no other period does man extol God's glory and omnipotence in such theatrical and richly endowed expressions.

TEMPLES TODAY

"Three things are needed for beauty: wholeness, harmony and radiance." (Thomas Aquinas)

As in the past, the Church of today must be conceived primarily as an arena of gathering for prayer with specific reference to man's present beliefs and understandings. The contemporary Church must however still evolve and develop from the great heritage of its past, where, in the words of Pope John Paul II *"the functional is always wedded to the creative impulse, inspired by a sense of the beautiful and an intuition of the mystery"*. In the modern church, these qualities must still be manifest, but they must now be brought together in a fusion that combines and integrates them with present theologies and their relative interpretations. However, grasping the spirit of the new theology may not always be easy. Since the very beginning of this century, the Church as an institution, has taken various steps towards eliminating the long standing separation between clergy and public; a separation resulting not only from imposed hierarchical segregation but also from the traditional Greek Cross plan form of churches with its clear divide between presbytery and nave. Pope Pius X's Papal Decree of 1903 planted the initial seeds for the faithful to no longer remain spectators but actively participate as co-celebrants. Post World War I movements in Germany continued developments in this direction. These changes were finally crystallized in the work of Pope John XXIII and Pope Paul VI with the publication of the Ecumenical Council document Vatican II, in 1963. This dossier clearly indicated the functional and liturgical requirements of the modern Church as a prayer space and opened the way to both modifying existing churches and conditioning the new. While before, the church building had remained above all an institution in which certain rituals were performed to an audience, it was now to be considered essentially as a communication arena. The church of the Third Millennium must therefore primarily read as a place of welcome and convocation. The new prayer spaces are not to be conceived as houses of God; nor as some pre-echo of heaven, but more tangibly, as places of convergence and dialogue between God and man. The Church as the community of the faithful must now be the place where the words of Christ *"when two or three meet together in My name, I will be amongst them"* become manifest. The function of a church building today is to bring people forward to meet with God in a space where the Word of God is heard, prayer is accomplished and man's spirit and relationship with God is rejuvenated. The main object and focus must remain that of re-energizing this sense of gathering and community. The contemporary church must ultimately be seen as a locus where sacred time and sacred space are brought together to evoke the ritual of eternal presence.

Religion will always continue to endure into man's future existence affirming mankind's vulnerability despite advanced scientific knowledge. In fact, no amount of increased scientific knowledge or economic efficiency can ever satisfy the needs of the soul. Religion fills the void that material comfort cannot, but it must keep adapting itself to the changing times. The Rock on which the Church was founded remains the same but its historical reality and its material and concrete contemporality must be in a constant state of change to keep pace with the world. Paraphrasing Dostoievsky, the words of Kikko Arguello, founder of the Neocatechumenal Way state that *"only a new aesthetic will save the Church"*. Richard Bergmann, an architect who has devoted much time to the study of the theme of contemporary sacrality, has written that *"using historical architectural styles is a lie. Our concern must be to clothe the truths of faith in honest modern dress. It is better to come in front of God naked than in period costume."* The new Liturgy is still anchored to the dogmatic principles of faith, but it is now modified to respond better to contemporary needs and understanding.

Our current concepts of heaven and hell and that of our reading of God have undergone radical changes. God is no longer contemplated as an old man with a white beard and a stick, and heaven is certainly no longer a place, well past Beatrice's vision of its urbanity in Dante's Divine Comedy or Milton's account of Paradise characterized by walls and other urban elements. Pope John Paul II himself has recently told us that heaven cannot be thought of in physical or temporal terms. It is not a place in the clouds, but neither is it an abstraction. Heaven is today conceived as a state of being; the manifestation of a living and personal relationship of union with the Holy Spirit. Consequently, hell also cannot be pictured in physical or temporal terms, but is now thought of as the cryptic agony and ominous despair of the total segregation and separation from God.

Having briefly outlined the concepts and the requirements which need to be integrated in the making of a contemporary church, one must now raise the question as to how an architect is to approach the problem of dealing with these and how one manifests these needs in built-form. As the last days of the 20th Century passed into the dawn of the new Millennium, it cannot but be admitted that this has been an age where spiritual values have all but been overcome by the overwhelming materialistic overlay of our living patterns. Despite the fact that the past Century has provided great and significant strides in the field of scientific knowledge and communications, man still knows least about what matters most. It seems that we live in an age where we know the price of everything and the value of nothing ! The problem of the contemporary concept of sacredness and that of bringing God into the Third Millennium becomes even more complex in today's secular society. God today has strong competition. The Church must offer dynamic responses to the current mass-media barrage of radical confrontation. How then does an architect utilize the readily available sophisticated technologies together with his own technical and artistic qualities to produce pasture places of prayer which are not only relevant to today, but are also crowd-pullers which are attractive and conducive to a public long brain-washed by contemporary high-tech commercial methodologies ? Perhaps a return to bare essentials, a process of the elimination of the non-essential, is a step in the right direction. "Less is more" is a good axiom. This approach would certainly serve as a welcome antidote to my native land's long-prevailing ostentatious culture of a Baroque typology where simplicity is thought of in terms of poverty and more is never enough !

To create areas of prayer, one must also of necessity create arenas of beauty. *"It is useful because it is beautiful"* writes Antoine de Saint Exupery in his classic tale *"The Little Prince"*. Numerous great thinkers have expressed thoughts on this theme. St. Augustine himself defines beauty in almost architectural terms as the *"splendour of order"*. Dostoievsky believed that the world could be saved by beauty and that Christ is Beauty. Others like the 20th Century theologian Hans Urs von Balthasar, whose writings on theological aesthetics constitute a deep and profound thesis, equates beauty to glory, and refers specifically to a *"cosmic liturgy"*. Simone Weil, on the other hand, firmly states that *"beauty is the only way for contemporary man to arrive at belief in God."* It seems therefore a logical conclusion to reach, that if God is Beauty, the Church, as transmitter of His presence, must also be conceived in beauty.

In this field of activity, the architect is primarily concerned with the creation of a place which is to serve as a refuge for the soul. It was Axel Munthe who reminded us that *"the soul needs more space than the body"*. In the making of the contemporary church there are some who believe that the technical and professional abilities of the architect may be sufficient in the fulfilling of his task. Followers of this theory think that these assets together with correct solutions to the purely functional problems of the building could, on their own, produce adequate places of prayer. To see well, to hear well are obvious necessities; but on their own may well produce nothing more than an auditorium; still-born and lifeless in as far as spiritual content is concerned. On the other hand, I believe, as my mentor and teacher Gio Ponti had taught me in my student days that *"religious architecture is not a matter of architecture, but a matter of religion"*. In order to produce a house in which man meets God in communion, it is, I am convinced, necessary for the architect to annexe to his secular architectural tools, not only the poetic, but more so the sacred tool of faith. It is through the passage of prayer that this faith is reached. *"If the Lord is not helping the builders, then the building of a house is to no purpose."* (Psalm 127:1)

THE ARCHITECT IN SEARCH OF THE SACRED

I have always considered myself particularly fortunate and privileged in my career as an architect, to have been involved with the design and building of many churches and prayer spaces.

My body of work of religious spaces spreads over four decades and may be divided into three categories comprising private prayer spaces, houses for the dead and public prayer arenas. In all these, the challenge focuses on the manifestation of space as 'sacred' and its transition and distinction from surrounding 'secular' areas. I have noted with particular interest that as these spaces are transfigured into prayer places, they also become arenas which forge the transfiguration of their users. As more prayer is offered within their walls, the spaces become more conducive to and accessible vehicles for future acts of prayer.

PRIVATE PRAYER PLACES

"Every life needs its altar. It may be in a church or quiet nook, it may be a moment in the day, or a mood of the heart... but somewhere the spiritual life must have its altar. From there, life gains its poise and direction." (Esther B. York)

For the design of exiguous small-scale sacred areas, the architect is particularly privileged in as far that he has almost clear-cut Divine instructions in relation to requirements, as handed down in the Gospel of Matthew. Christ's clear directions in the words *"go into your inner room, close the door and pray"* evoke images of private secluded areas where man can dialogue with his Creator in environments of solitude and peace. Matthew proceeds to report that Christ continued with the words *"Pray to the Father. He is there in silence"*. This, together with other references in the Holy Book to Christ in prayer, emphasizes His preference for solitary environments and secluded places in His choice of locations. We find Him indulging in prayer either on far away mountain-tops or walking in isolated composure on sands of desert emptiness; spaces always reduced to the ultimate essentials, where the floor is the earth, the walls are the wind and the ceiling is the sky. Everywhere the emphasis is on solitude and silence. The architect, therefore, in creating private prayer spaces, must conceive these environments as places in which one can stop and pause; places where one must be silent and unspoken to. The pianist Arthur Schnabel once said *"the notes I play like any other pianist, but the silences in between... that is where the secret is"*.

The problem continues to focus on the non-facile process of transition of secular space into sacred space. The necessity of a threshold as a meditative bridge and rite of passage between these two areas remains paramount. One cannot approach sacred areas casually; transition as understood in terms of a pathway of preparation for arrival, is in itself a process of ritual for eventual communication between humans and the transcendent. If faith is the ultimate tool in the manifestation of a sacred place, honesty, simplicity and reverence are the stepping stones to manifest this belief in built-form. Above all, this becomes the architect's search for essence and meaning. In the making of these minimal areas of prayer, I believe an architect must seek to achieve

places of silence

in spaces of solitude

enclosed by walls of mysticism.

The silence attained

must be one that speaks and not muted.

The solitude raised

should be one of communion

and not loneliness.

While the mysticism endorsed

must extend beyond man's mortal senses

to reach his inner eternal spirit.

Then, and only then

will the manifest religious architecture become the threshold

between the realm of the materialistic and the spiritual:

the doorway to establish a dialogue of prayer

between the ordinariness of man

and the infinity of God.

In such works the challenge remains the creation of an exalted form of silence, a silence which in itself must not be permitted to become loud but which provides the necessary sense of companionship with the Divine. Silence defined by Malcolm Quantrill as *"architecture's fifth dimension"*, here functions as a purifying agent; a refuge and retreat in muted tones from the spiritually bankrupt world of today. Philosophy is descriptive but architecture, with its spatial enclosures within defined walls, provides distinct direct experience. The architect, as creator of these spaces, is here acting in his highest capacity as mood manipulator, designing spaces and creating worlds of shadowland to integrate body, mind and spirit; therapeutic healing spaces for the soul.

THE TEMPLE IN THE HOUSE

"Buildings are also homes for the soul." (Urlik Plesner)

In the design of the contemporary domestic habitat the architect must provide solutions on numerous materialistic levels. The requirements of the client will provide him with a brief particular to the individual's needs. While every aspect of human activity is considered and attended to in the design of the human dwelling, it has always puzzled me as to why no importance is ever given to the requirements of the spiritual side of man. Ergonomics and standardized patterns lay out rules to provide solutions to materialistic problems. The house of today is not only a dwelling place, but also due to recent technological advances it is fast also becoming man's working arena. While we allocate spaces for each of our human activities with great care, little or no attention is given to spaces for the rejuvenation of the spirit. Surely in today's fast-moving mechanized world it is time that the habitat of man encompasses meditative healing spaces and some form of a sacred space. These would help in providing solace and quiet-time for the soul to catch up with the body. Since the sacred is thought of as the most intimate part of man, surely he should have it readily available and close at hand within his normal everyday ambiance. Initially the concept of personal meditative prayer spaces may be looked upon as a luxury. With their repeated use, however, and the solace they donate, they gradually transcend themselves into a need and eventually to a necessity for inside each person lurks a yearning for and a vision of a personal sacred place. Concealed under the turmoil of daily concerns this basic necessity manifests itself as the vital aspiration for replenishment and healing of contemporary man's physical and spiritual aspects. Without faith and belief life is but an apocalyptic cul de sac. *"Unless you believe, you shall not understand."* (Isaiah)

HOUSES FOR THE DEAD

"Doorways to be entered only once." (Alain Resnais)

The quest for life beyond life and man's unwillingness to accept the finality of death are linked through the ages by attitudes assumed by both primitive and advanced societies. Houses for the dead seem to provide us with more information about the living habits of a society than that made available through the houses of the living. Since man seems to spend more time in his final resting habitat than in any house for the living, it is not surprising that from the earliest of time humans have dedicated much effort and respect to the individual tomb or the collective city of the dead, the Necropolis. The object of an architecture of death in Christian terminology is to demonstrate the belief in a continuing existence of the departed in the minds of the still-living, and more so in the creed of resurrection and immortality. The tomb may, in a way, be interpreted as an architecture of absence, but the Christian faith provides a beacon of light at the end of the tunnel. From the practical point of view of the architect, this category of building may be said to provide the designer with an almost total absence of practical problems as the user-client seems unlikely to raise complaints about leaking roofs or penetration of damp!

On a more elevated level, the architect in this context must again seek to discover the essential meaning and essence of the typology of the house of the dead. Perhaps the archetypal image of a burial space injected with the necessary undertones of essentiality and sparsity is to be found in a Pompeian Tomb, which emerged from under the cinderous volcanic ashes after almost two thousand years of sepulchral oblivion. It consists of a circular seat around the grave; an invitation to pause to resume a conversation with a loved one, begun on earth. A locus, pregnant with poignancy, to carry on an interrupted dialogue. What can you add ? Architects would do well to discard the rampant self-glorifying monumental neo-classicism so often utilized in funerary architecture and follow the clarity and essentiality of this Pompeian model. In the words of Aulis Blomstedt, *"restraint is the privilege of the great."*

PUBLIC PRAYER PLACES

"One seeks God in books, one finds Him in prayer." (Padre Pio)

The requirements for large public spaces involve the architect in a very different task. Public prayer is perhaps closer to an activated form of a structured liturgical ritual. Therefore, while exiguous prayer spaces have the possibility to be more organic, protective and contemplative, large public worship areas tend to develop in a more rigorous and formal manner. The memory of Eden's primordial perfection with its structured layout, four streams and two magical trees becomes the most sought after paradigm of perfection, and points strongly to an archetypal order of sacred geometry. Although, as we have stated before, the Church, post Vatican II, has shed many of its hierarchical barriers and the emphasis is now on creating that essential sense of gathering and community in the celebration of the Eucharistic Meal; in prayer spaces of considerable size, a professional layering of the building, formalism and solemnization must still prevail, if only to ensure order. The Eucharistic celebration at the altar table, the reading of the Word of God at the ambone and the pouring of water in the ritual of Baptism, form the basic triad of the Catholic Liturgy. It is logical therefore, that in the design of contemporary churches the emphasis is on these arenas of liturgical activities as it is also on the ever-present need of symbolism. Man today is less in need of a recounted or visual narrative and the culture of the time becomes more dependent of the reading of symbolic echoes. The Church today, as an institution, must dedicate much of its time and toil to the life pattern and development of its community. Much of its efforts, outside the walls of the actual gathering spaces, must focus on the problems of youth, family and the elderly. This concern and care must be interpreted as a direct development of the advances made in recent years in modern anthropology and sociology. The Church as a parish has, as its main contemporary objective, the training of man and the making of the complete human being. It must therefore extend its work parameters to human and conciliatory levels on a wider social scale. As science continues to advance, it may well, in the future, answer all the questions relating to man's existence in terms of when or where. As to the why, that will remain essentially the realm of religion.

CONCLUSION

"Inside my empty bottle I was constructing a lighthouse, while others were making ships." (C.S. Lewis)

In the making of both private and public prayer spaces, the architect must consider himself privileged in having the opportunity of creating places for that very special communion between man and his Creator. Ultimately, what the spaces give back will depend on the love and commitment which the architect and the builders have put into their making. Mother Teresa's words *"it is not so much the doing, but how much love you put into the doing"* emphasize this equation. The transformation of material space designed by the architect into sacred space takes place when a conversational dialogue together with a thread of prayer between man and God are established and manifested. As the material buildings transcend themselves into sacred spaces, it is then that the real objective is achieved. The bridge of prayer will transform these arenas into sanctuaries for the soul and the materials utilized in the buildings now illuminated with the breath of the Holy Spirit will become the transmitters of the Good News of the Word of God. The architect provides the water. The sanctification of these spaces will change this water into wine. In this Divine manifestation, the architect can only sit back in humility and thank his Creator for the unique and blessed privilege of being a small part of this great miracle.

"O gracious and holy Father,
give us wisdom to perceive You,
intelligence to understand You,
diligence to seek You,
the patience to wait for You,
eyes to see You,
a heart to meditate on You,
and a life to proclaim You through the
power of the spirit of Jesus Christ our Lord."

St. Benedict.

PLACES OF PRAYER

HOME CHAPEL

When I came to the entrance of the chapel, I paused on the threshold, unsure of what stopped me. Then I realised I needed to be barefoot and vulnerable and more open to experience the grace of this holy place. Drawn in, I had an almost tangible sensation of being cleansed as I came.

"Come to me, all you who are weary and burdened, and I will give you rest." (Matthew 11:28)

Lord Jesus, I feel Your welcome in this gentle place of quiet rest. Receiving me in love, You invite me to come right up to You and drop my burdens at the foot of Your cross. Your Spirit whispers to my fragile soul. "Peace, My precious one. Abide in Me and absorb My strength. Invite into your heart My Holy Spirit, the burden-bearer. My gift to you is rest, a centre of quiet in the midst of unrest. My gift to you is peace, that holds your trembling heart in the midst of turmoil. My gift to you is Me. I Myself will be for you all you need Me to be. Come to Me and ask for help and I will be there. I will be with you always, in all ways. I love you."

Linda Schubert

A sacred space installed in a home provides that home with the unique gift of a soul.

Richard England

M.U.S.E.U.M. CHAPEL, BLATA L-BAJDA

As I entered this chapel through a dark narrow hallway, my first sensation was a desire to flee. My own preference is for open spaces. Here I felt disturbed, caged, conflicted. Challenged to see something I didn't want to look at, my only desire was to turn and run. When I surrendered to the Lord's grace in this place and faced the inner turmoil, I became open to a transforming encounter with God Himself.

"You will know the truth, and the truth will set you free." (John 8:32)

Lord Jesus, in the surprising power of this holy room I hear Your words of deliverance: "Beloved, allow Me to reach past the dark prisons of your bondage and lift you into the truth of My love. You come expecting scolding and I immerse you in My unconditional love. Choose life, and your heavy soul will soar on wings of joy. My gift to you is freedom. I release you from the tight structures that bind you. I release you from your need to measure up to a standard I did not impose on you. I release you. I release you. I release you. I am the way, the truth and the life. Choose My truth and the chains will be shattered. I offer you My freedom and a fresh understanding of My gift to you. I love you."

Linda Schubert

A cavern-like chapel inspired by man's earliest locus of prayer: a space which evokes warmth, shelter and a sense of protection.

Richard England

M.U.S.E.U.M. MEDITATION CHAPEL, NAXXAR

There was a feeling of openness and freedom in the approach to the chapel. Upon entering, I sat close to the altar, very low, near the floor, hugged my knees and rocked back and forth. I felt an overwhelming welcome, and this made me vulnerable. Concealing my face to hide a flow of unexpected tears, I wanted to remain for hours.

"For God so loved the world that He gave His one and only Son, that whoever believes in Him shall not perish but have eternal life." (John 3:16)

Lord Jesus, in the silent rhythm of this sanctuary of hope I hear Your timeless voice penetrating my heart: 'I love you. I love you. I love you. My Father's love sent Me to bring you into our family. Open your heart to My love and to My world. My love takes you beyond self-preoccupation. My love comforts you beyond your need, beyond your fear, bringing new life, new light, new love. Hear My love resounding through you and echoing around the world. My gift to you is My extravagant heart. My love gift to you goes on and on and on, without limit. I love you.'

Linda Schubert

A sacred space providing a silence which is not muted but one that speaks and a solitude which is not one of loneliness but of communion.

Richard England

FRANCISCAN CHAPEL, BURMARRAD

In this little tilting chapel, familiarity embraced me like a dear friend who knew the worst and best of me and loved me through it all. I felt relaxed, docile and vulnerable, and so very much in need of healing. I also knew I was in the presence of my Healer.

"He took up our infirmities and carried our sorrows... and by His wounds we are healed." (Isaiah 53:4-5)

Lord Jesus, this little sacred space brings forth amazement that You would want to help me, with all my imperfections. In my tears of gratitude, I hear Your clear words of hope: "Beloved, the twisted and fearful places in your life are mirrored by this room. Look to the light beyond the cross. Light is My resurrection love that takes you beyond brokenness into wholeness. Come with Me, beyond the cross. Let Me give you a higher perspective. My gift to you is the view from the resurrection side of the cross. My gift to you is hope. My gift to you is life. I love you."

Linda Schubert

Focussing on the light beyond the Cross as a symbol of Christ's resurrection, this minimal prayer space provides a beacon reflecting also the Christian belief in an eternal afterlife.

Richard England

SANDRINA'S CHAPEL, MGARR

This chapel seemed at first like a desert enclosed by walls. All my familiar props were stripped away. In the discomfort I kept searching for something to nurture me. Even the cross was austere. A dramatic removal from the familiar had to take place before I could hear the fatherly voice of the Shepherd.

"I am the Good Shepherd, I know My sheep and My sheep know Me." (John 10:14)

Lord Jesus, in the stark simplicity of this chapel of abandonment I hear You whisper, "Precious child, I am your Shepherd. I love you too much to leave you where you are. Will you allow Me to remove the non-essentials from your life ? I want to restore the real you. Permit Me to guide you through the emotional hills and valleys of your life, and lead you to the truth of who you are. Allow Me to shepherd your soul beyond your fears into living faith that has no room for fear. Let Me shepherd your whole nature into a healthy way of living. I want you to know Me deeply, as I know you. I want you to know the real you, through My eyes. Knowing yourself and knowing Me is My gift to you. I love you."

Linda Schubert

Hewn into the earth rock, this chapel reflects my search for the sacred through a process of the elimination of the non-essential. The threshold of rough pebbles acts as a form of cleansing in the passage between secular and sacred areas.

Richard England

DAR IL-HANIN SAMARITAN, SANTA VENERA

Tears burst forth as I walked into the centre of this chapel of light. The burning brilliance was laser beams in my soul, penetrating and loosening deep deposits of uncried tears, unspoken fears. The light of Christ was in this sacred place.

"I have come into this world as a light, so that no one who believes in Me should stay in darkness." (John 12:46)

Lord Jesus, You are the lovelight that floods this sanctuary. Creation power flows through Your words proclaimed in authority over my trembling form: "Let there be light. Let My light banish the fear and unbelief that lurks in the cellars of your mind. Let My light wash the sin, sorrow and shame from your soul. Let My light drive out disease and distress from your body. Let My light guide you through your grief and sorrow and loneliness into a place of peace and fresh faith. Light is My gift to you. Be filled with My lovelight, for you are so very deeply loved."

Linda Schubert

A celebration of light, the intensity of which continuously changes with the passing hours of the day. In this space one is able to pray bathed and washed in a joy of luminance.

Richard England

PUBLIC PRAYER SPACES

PAPAL PAVILIONS

To celebrate means to honour by ceremony and to mark by festivities. There seems to be a deep need in people's hearts to celebrate. Christians often experience moments of transfiguration as they gather as a celebrating assembly to honour Jesus Christ. This is another kind of prayer experience, a social one, that can awaken an individual to the need for more time in solitary prayer. When Catholics provide an elaborate staging for a visit by the Pope, for example, with colourful display and music and procession, they are honouring, through His representative, our Lord Jesus Christ. This is reason to celebrate, and an opportunity to pray for our spiritual leaders, perhaps something like this:

"Lord, we thank You for those You have chosen to lead us in our spiritual lives. We ask Your blessing upon them. May Your wisdom guide them, and Your love flow through them. Please help us to encourage them and support them as they strive to fulfil the role You have given them. Amen."

Linda Schubert

A series of colourful stage-sets conceived as choreographic back-drops for the public Masses celebrated by Pope John Paul II during his visit to the Maltese Islands in 1990. A transient architecture of celebration and festivity.

Richard England

CHURCH OF ST JOSEPH, MANIKATA

On several occasions during my visits to Malta I have seen on a distant hill the Church of St Joseph in Manikata. I was drawn to the church, and wanted to make a visit, but the opportunity never arose. My reflections arise from these brief glimpses and the yearning that those glimpses stirred. In my spirit I can hear the Lord beckoning: "As you come up to My holy hill, let it be a Mount of Transfiguration for you. As I was transfigured by My Father on Mount Horeb, My face *"shone like the sun"*. He said to My companions, *'This is My Son whom I love; with Him I am well pleased.'*"

I feel the Lord would have us each go up our holy mountain, whether it be the Church of Manikata or another high and sacred place, and allow Him to make a deep spiritual change in us - to give us a new heart and a face that shines like the "Son". He invites us to accept ourselves as His beloved sons and daughters, with whom He is well pleased, and to accept others in the same way.

Linda Schubert

Designed in 1962, this church became a symbol of a new spirit. Its innovative forms however, still recalled its origins and background, making it very much a church for today designed on the foundations of yesterday. It was my intention that the building was to be read more as a house for the community than one for the Deity.

Richard England

CHURCH OF ST FRANCIS OF ASSISI, QAWRA

During my first visit to the Church of St Francis, when it was still under construction, I ran to Richard England and whispered, *"I feel like marching up and down the aisle waving flags."* He smiled and pointed to a wall in the back that was to eventually hold a row of banners. Oh, I really love this church. Some churches draw people deeply inward, as in a warm dark womb, like probably the Church of St Joseph in Manikata would do. That has its own wonder and its own healing power. Here, I can forget about myself and with a certain abandon, wave flags and shout *"Praise You, Jesus, You are the King of Kings. Praise You, Jesus, You are the Lord of Lords."* This is also transfiguration.

Linda Schubert

Large public worship areas have of necessity to develop in a more rigorous and formal manner than exiguous prayer spaces. The layout of the church draws its organisational geometry from a series of inter-locking triangular and semi-circular forms which may also be read as a symbol of the Trinity. The internal spaces focus on the main altar where a figure of Christ floats in risen glory from the Cross behind it.

Richard England

CHAPELS OF REPOSE

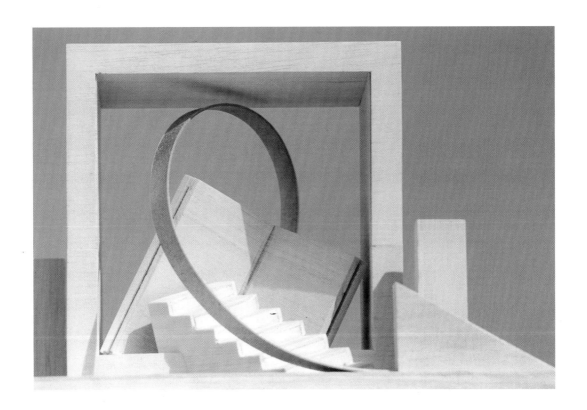

CHAPELS OF REPOSE

Christians believe in life after death. We believe our greatest moment of transfiguration comes when we leave our earthly bodies and unite with our Lord Jesus Christ. *"God is love,"* (1 Jn 4:16) and as we seek throughout our lives to respond to that love, we can look forward with anticipation to being united with (and thus transfigured by) Perfect Love. As Catholic Christians we believe we remain spiritually connected to our loved ones even in death, and that we can pray for them, asking Jesus to draw them closer to Himself. It is important to honour them, as God's children and as relatives God has given to us. The Catholic tradition of offering masses for the dead is the purest way of praying for our deceased loved ones. In our time of personal reflection, whether we are visiting a memorial chapel created to honour a loved one, or at their graveside, or simply alone with the Lord, we might pray something like this: "Thank You, Lord Jesus, for my family history. Thank You for the generations of Christians gone before me who have helped me to become who I am today. Thank You that none of us stand alone. Thank You for my mother and father, grandfathers and grandmothers, down through the line. Lord, in Your infinite mercy, please extend Your loving, healing blessings through the ages to everyone in my family line. Thank You for each one of them. Amen."

Linda Schubert

Houses for the dead may be read as a manifestation of the Christian belief in the creed of resurrection and immortality.

Richard England

ILPAĊI MIEGHEK

MAKING THE SPACES FRUITFUL

PRAYER

Most of these "prayer starters" will help people of all faiths; a few will describe how a Christian might pray. All readers are encouraged to reflect with openness, because each theme will help to awaken the sacred and bring life to the soul.

GRATITUDE

Gratitude promotes trust in God and trust in God opens the spirit. Spend a few moments being grateful for your life. Taking inventory of all the things we can be grateful for is a powerful way of bringing life into perspective. Say: "Lord, I want to live and pray with a heart of thanksgiving." Start with two things from the past, two things from the present and two things you expect in the future and begin to form a habit of gratitude. In time you will pray with gratitude in even the most difficult areas of your life. Habitual gratitude will benefit all areas of life.

PRAISE

Praising God draws us into His presence. For Christians, spending a few moments praising God helps them get past self-centredness and releases an area of the personality that is turned inward. They might pray: "Praise You Lord, You are my helper. When I am in need You are there to intervene and take my side. Praise You Lord, You are my Counsellor. When I don't know what to do, You give me Your wisdom and help me see things clearly. Praise You, Lord, You give me Your love for the ones I have trouble loving. Praise You Lord, You are the One who gives peace in the midst of the storm. Praise You Lord, You are my Deliverer. When trouble comes, You draw me under Your wing and protect me as a mother hen gathers her chicks. As I praise You, my heart and mind awaken to Your holy presence and I see things in a higher and better way. Help me to continue to praise You. Amen."

SURRENDER

Expressing total dependency on God does something glorious for the human spirit. As we yield our hearts and just let God love us, life will shift into balance. Health, growth and fruitfulness begin to flow. Pray something like this: "God, I entrust my life into Your care. I surrender to You with all my heart, just as I am. I give You the longings of my soul, the unsatisfied dreams, the failures. I give You all of me - past, present and future - the best and the worst. In faith and trust, I let go of everything so I can hold onto You. Help me to be all You want me to be. In sickness and in health, in life and in death, I choose to belong to You. Thank You for loving me. Amen."

THE HOLY SPIRIT

The Christian recognises the gift and ministry of the Holy Spirit. He is the connection to Jesus and the ability to respond to what God wants. He enables Christians to sing in their sorrow and move forward when they have no strength. Through the Holy Spirit, Christians experience the love of Jesus in a powerful way. In the New Testament, Romans 5:5 says *"the love of God is poured into our hearts by the Holy Spirit who is given to us."* Christians are encouraged to spend a few moments praying something like this: "Come Holy Spirit and fill me with the love of God in every area of my life, including the deep, painful and fearful parts. Let Your love empower me to live and love in healthy and life-giving ways and bring me close to Jesus. Amen."

SELF-EXAMINATION

As we open our lives to God we begin to recognise areas that need to be transformed. Everyone has secret spots they don't want anyone to see, especially if they believe God is a policeman or a judge. This is a holy moment of trust, where we could pray something like this: "Lord, I am sorry for offending You by blocking Your love in my life. Please show me any areas in my life that are out of order. I repent of my sins, faults and failings and turn away from all things that are destructive and harmful. Lord, I give You those areas I'm most ashamed of - secret guilt, hateful thoughts, pretenses, things I've neglected to do. Help me to acknowledge wrongs and take responsibility for any needed correction. Lead me on Your path of virtue where my conscience is sensitized to recognize and respond to Your love. Thank You Lord. Amen."

FORGIVENESS

Human beings all know, in the depths of their soul, the inherent need to forgive and be forgiven. They are continually faced with injustices and their own weaknesses, faults and failings. Our words often shatter relationships and build barriers. Christians acknowledge Jesus as the one who gives courage to forgive wrongs, and they turn to the Holy Spirit as their enabler. In making a decision to be reconciled with people, we might pray something like this: "Lord, because You have forgiven me, I choose to forgive everyone in my life. I forgive my mother and father for hurts they inflicted. I forgive my spouse for unloving actions. I forgive my children, sisters and brothers, relatives, friends and employers. I forgive teachers, clergy and every person of influence in my life. I choose to forgive each one, especially the one causing pain right now. Because You have forgiven me, I forgive myself, especially for things I am the most ashamed of. Lord please bless those who have hurt me and bring Your peace to my heart. Show me how to express Your love to each one. Thank You Lord. Amen."

SACRED WRITING

Of the many tools God uses to awaken His people, sacred writings are one of the most powerful. For Christians, the Bible opens wonderful doors to God's holy presence. In the Bible, God the Father is revealed as the creator and sustainer of life. Out of His love, everything proceeds. God the Son, Jesus Christ, comes to us as our loving Saviour to reveal and impart the character and nature of God. The Holy Spirit was given to unite us to Jesus and enable us to live in Him. Many Christians find the Bible to be the greatest avenue of interaction with Jesus. As a part of daily prayer, Christians are invited to begin by reading a chapter or a few verses in the Gospel of John, the Acts of the Apostles and/or the Psalms. As we read the Bible with the desire to know and love the Lord better, we often find Him awakening our spirit to hear Him speak. God is love and love communicates. His words, spoken deep in our heart, will be words of love and encouragement. You might begin this way: "Lord, thank You for Your words in the Bible. Open my spirit as I read Your sacred writing. I want to know You and love You even as You know and love me."

PRAYING FOR SELF

As we become aware of the wonderful presence of God we discover to our amazement that we are precious to Him. This awareness softens our soul and makes us docile to His nature coming alive in us. It becomes easier to bring every concern to Him. Seek to know how valuable you are to God, and form a habit of asking Him for everything. Ask Him for food, for help with physical, emotional, social, financial needs. Even though we are used to thinking we provide these things for ourselves, everything is a gift from God.

PRAYING FOR OTHERS

As our sense of the sacred unfolds we begin to awaken to the needs of others with surprising generosity. There will also emerge a growing awareness of both the privilege of praying for others and an increasing ability to do so effectively. Spend a few moments praying for other people each day. Start with those nearest and dearest, then as your heart grows, expand your requests to include others around the world. Pray for the youth, for marriages, for families, for the homeless, the forgotten. Ask the Lord to bless them, forgive them, help them, heal them and touch them with His love. As we continue to speak to God on behalf of others, our spirit begins to flourish.

MORE GRATITUDE

Fill yourself with spontaneous gratitude. Close your prayer time as you began, with your life wrapped in loving thankfulness. Say: "Thank You, God, for awakening in me the sense of Your presence. Thank You for increasing my gratitude and my desire to praise You. Thank You for giving me the desire to surrender my life into Your care. Thank You for the grace to face the things in my life that are out of order, and make necessary changes. Thank You for teaching me how to love. Thank You for enabling me to receive Your forgiveness and be open to reconciliation. Thank You for sacred writings and enlarging my heart to pray for others. Thank You for meeting all of my needs. Thank You for wanting me to know You. I am grateful for the life You have given me. I accept it as a gift from You. I love You God. Amen."

Linda Schubert

THE TEMPLE IN THE HOUSE

THE TEMPLE IN THE HOUSE

After experiencing the power of Richard's chapels in Malta, I realized how much I needed a more focussed prayer space at home. Because my home is small and simple, what I have done is to create a little portable altar that I set on my coffee table in the early hours of the morning. It includes an image of Jesus, a crucifix and a candle, on a small platform draped in deep purple.

The imporant thing I have discovered is that I need a place to focus my attention. Without that point of concentration, it is easy to wander and become distracted. With that centre of attention it is easier to pray. Along with that focus of attention, I need a place that is uncluttered and peaceful and attractive.

Whatever the prayer space is, it needs to be clean and simple with only images and things that draw the person into prayer. These will vary with the individual. But it all comes back again to *"focus"*. That is why it is so ideal to have a space that is used only for prayer. When it is a space used only for prayer, dedicated to that singular purpose, it becomes increasingly easy to pray in that location. It seems to build, as if filling the room with a heavenly presence. *"You will show me the path to life, fullness of joys in your presence."* (Psalm 16:11)

Linda Schubert

Locating a sacred space in one's home helps, above all, to give the house a soul. It will also give to the life of the people who dwell within its walls meaning, solace and a sense of wholeness; essential qualities in the fragmented patterns of our confused contemporary style of living.

A sacred locus will provide a recuperative arena to spend quiet time to find oneself. It was Joseph Campbell who said *"sacred space is where you find yourself again and again."* These areas transform themselves into spaces of spiritual re-generation. *"My house shall be called a house of prayer."* (Matt 21:13) Moments spent in prayer provide a much needed time frame for renewal.

Readers are encouraged to locate a space in their home for this most necessary form of spiritual healing. Silence, order and an away from it all feeling are paramount. The space may be a minimal one but, above all, it should be harmonious, intimate and private as the most essential feed-back that one should get from it is that it allows one to focus solely on the activity of prayer. Prayer requires total concentration and commitment and the space chosen for man to give homage to his Creator must provide no distraction.

It is augured that the pages of this publication will provide inspiration for the creation of private temples in the home for both the maintenance and more essentially, the replenishment and rejuvination of the human spirit.

Richard England

AFTERWORD

AFTERWORD

Space can be sacred or secular. A space can serve a sacred purpose, for prayer for example, as Richard England's sacred spaces do. Or, a space can serve a secular purpose. The sacred-secular distinction is this: whatever refers directly to God in its purpose is sacred; whatever does not refer directly to God in its purpose is secular. The chalice used in the Mass is sacred; a coffee cup is secular. A monk has a sacred calling; a dentist has a secular calling.

Churches and chapels and prayer places are sacred spaces. Office buildings and kitchens are secular spaces. A prayer place in a home is a sacred space; a chapel or church is a sacred space.

The sacred places in this book are spaces set apart that refer directly to God, places to pray in, places to meet God, arenas of communion with God. Because they are prayer places, and so refer directly to God, they are sacred.

Richard England's sacred spaces are Christian, and they follow the principle of the Incarnation, that since God has become human, matter has become a proper vehicle for the spiritual. Certainly, sacred space helps to create particular moods, a sense of silence, of not-empty solitude, of dialogue and communion with God, of tranquility, peace, security, hope. Shape, space, colour, light and dark, help to form not a mute silence but a silence that speaks, and not a sense of aloneness but a climate of loving communion with God. The prayer places in this book can be said to make prayer incarnate. They are properly occasions of the grace of prayer, sacramentals of prayer, in the way that holy water or blessed salt or a blessing is an occasion of grace.

The sacred spaces in this book embody prayer. Each of these spaces possesses its own unique balance of light and shadow, of rest and movement, of presence and emptiness, of fullness and void, its own disposition of shapes and colours and shades. These places welcome the human in its encounter with the Divine. And this too mirrors the Incarnation.

Sacred spaces are not of course confined to Christianity. A synagogue is a sacred place. Zen gardens, Buddhist shrines, Hindu temples, mosques, are all sacred places. But Christian sacred spaces, and in a particular way those of Richard England, are especially rich in sacredness because of their sacramentality, their embodiment of prayer, and their icon-like quality of acting as occasions of grace.

Richard England's sacred spaces always have a threshold, a clearly marked passage into the sacred place. We cannot go instantaneously from daily secular activities into communion with God. We need a brief moment of recollection, of preparation, of coming more consciously into God's presence. We need a moment for passage from secular to sacred. This passage finds itself represented perhaps in a corridor from outside into a cavern-like sacred space, or in an atrium, or in a kind of screen to go through or around, or in some other type of material entrance place.

In another sense, Richard England's sacred places are themselves thresholds. They are places of contact between us and God, places of passage between this world and the world to come, between this life and eternal life. They do not belong to secular reality. They open out into the next world. This fact is often symbolized in Richard England's public chapels and churches by light, a metaphor for salvation and for heaven, coming from behind the altar or the cross. In the more private small places of prayer eternal life is symbolized, represented, by the sense of security and of finding a safe haven in an often almost cave-like atmosphere.

This threshold quality of the sacred is called *"liminality"*, from the Latin *"limen"* or *"threshold"*. A threshold stands between two places or two rooms or two stages. A liminal activity or state or place is *"neither here nor there"*; it *"falls between the cracks"* of the secular structures of society; it is marginal to secular structures or underneath them or above them. What is liminal stands apart from regular secular societal structures.

The sacred is always liminal. What is sacred stands between this secular world and the world to come. It stands apart from profane reality, and it opens out into the life to come by referring directly to God and by representing and facilitating communion with Him. A priest, a monk, a nun, have liminal callings and live in a liminal state. A church, a temple, a synagogue, a meditation room, are all liminal.

Prayer is a liminal activity. A sacred space is a liminal place, set aside, not really fitting into secular structures, a place apart. Richard England's sacred spaces possess to a high degree the quality of liminality.

The characteristics of the sacred spaces in this book are:

1. Simplicity at the service of prayer.
2. Sacredness: they are spaces set apart for prayer, clearly different from and distinguishable from secular space.
3. Sacramentality: these places dispose us for graces of prayer; they act as occasions for graces of prayer, represent prayer, embody prayer.
4. Liminality: they stand above and outside society's secular structures.

Prayer is a spiritual experience, but not of course entirely spiritual. Christian prayer follows the principle of the Incarnation, that the Word has become flesh in Jesus. Christian prayer takes place; it has a material setting. Sacred spaces are particularly appropriate material contexts for prayer.

Posture is important. An appropriate posture not only symbolizes my lowliness, humility, reverence; it embodies, is, an act of humility before God, of reverence. Sitting in a chair in a reverent posture, or standing reverently, can serve as prayer postures. Particularly appropriate for prayer because they especially stand for and are reverence and humility before God are kneeling or sitting on the floor or rug or pad or low seat.
What should I do in a place of prayer ? Pray.

How can I pray ? I can use the *"prayer starters"* that Linda Schubert gives us in her *"Prayer"* section of this book. Or I can say or read a familiar prayer, such as the *"Our Father"*, very slowly, letting the words sink in, resting in each phrase, dwelling on each group of words and letting that phrase unite me to God.

Or I can read the Bible slowly and prayerfully, a Psalm for instance, or a brief section of one of the four gospels in the New Testament. The Gospel of John lends itself well to this kind of slow prayerful reading. I can read a verse or two, maybe even at random, and then rest in those few lines, resting in God and letting the words of the Bible unite me to Him.

After that, I can use centering prayer or something similar, for - say - about ten or fifteen minutes. In centering prayer, I put a short phrase in my heart and repeat it in my heart slowly and silently. The name of Jesus, for example. Very slowly let the word *"Jesus"* repeat itself in my heart. And I let that be my centre. I centre myself on the name of Jesus spoken silently and slowly in my heart, and through that centering on His holy name, I centre myself in faith on Jesus Himself. This kind of contemplation or Christian meditation is non-conceptual prayer, an especially fruitful and healing and unity-with-God way to pray.

The creation of a sacred space is a special gift of the Holy Spirit, a charism. New Testament examples of charisms are prophecy, healing, casting out evil spirits, the discernment of spirits, teaching, administering, leading. The Second Vatican Council speaks about charisms several times. In the document on the church it says, *"The Holy Spirit distributes charisms among the faithful of every rank; by these gifts He makes them fit and ready for various tasks or duties toward the renewal and up building of the church."* (The Dogmatic Constitution on the Church, Number 12).

An example of the charism of art is the making of icons. In the eastern Christian tradition of sacred art, the painting of icons has always been held as a special gift of the Holy Spirit, a particular grace, a charism. An icon is a painting only in the sense that the Bible is a book; an icon is more than just a painting. It is an inspired painting, a graced painting, a painting made in the Spirit. Icons have a sacramental effect. They tend to be occasions of *"the grace that they stand for,"* to lead the viewer to a closer union with whoever is depicted in the icon: the Trinity, Jesus, or Mary, or one of the saints.

There are Christian charisms of painting, of print making, of poetry or music. And of architecture.

Richard England's sacred spaces are architectural icons, conceived and put together in the Spirit. They lead to and facilitate what they represent: a closer prayerful union with God.

Robert Faricy, S.J.

BIOGRAPHICAL NOTES

RICHARD ENGLAND was born in Malta and graduated in Architecture at the University of Malta. He continued his studies in Italy at the Milan Polytechnic and also worked as a student-architect in the studio of the Italian architect-designer Gio Ponti.

He is also a sculptor, photographer, poet, painter and the author and subject of several books.

Richard England is a Visiting Professor at the University of Malta, a Professor (Honoris Causa) at the University of Buenos Aires, Argentina, and a Visiting Fellow at the University of Bath, in England. He is an Academician of the International Academy of Architecture. He is also a Professor (Honoris Causa) at the Institute of Advanced Studies at the University of New York, U.S.A. In 1993 the Government of Malta appointed him Officer of The Order of Merit and in 1999, he was appointed Hon. Fellow of the American Institute of Architects.

His buildings and designs have earned him numerous International Awards, including the Interarch '85 and Interarch '91 Laureate Prizes and two Commonwealth Association of Architects Regional awards in 1985 and 1987. Other awards include the "Comite Des Critiques d'Architecture" (C.I.C.A.) Silver Medal in 1987, the 1988 Georgia, U.S.S.R. Biennale Laureate Prize and an IFRAA - AIA Award in 1991 for the Chapel of St Andrew, Malta. In 1996 two of his chapel designs were awarded the International Prize at the III Architectural Bienal of Costa Rica.

He has worked in the capacity of Architectural Consultant to governmental and private institutions in many countries including his native Malta.

LINDA SCHUBERT was born and raised in California, and is a graduate of the University of San Francisco with a B.S. in business and human relations. A spiritual conversion experience following the death of a stepson gradually drew her into full time service in her Christian faith. A Catholic convert, she has a special fondness for ecumenical groups. She has written several books on prayer and healing topics, the most popular being *Miracle Hour*, with more than a million copies in print in twenty six languages. Other books include *The Healing Power of a Father's Blessing, Miracle Moments, Rich in Mercy*, and *Five Minute Miracles*. She has also co-authored books with a Catholic priest. Today, Linda travels internationally conducting seminars and retreats and speaking at Christian conferences. She has given the keynote address at national Catholic conferences in Belize in Central America and in New Zealand, as well as the international conference of the Magnificat Ministry to Catholic Women in New Orleans, Louisiana. Her work has taken her to such countries as New Zealand, Australia, South Africa, Nigeria, the Caribbean, Germany, Poland, Italy, Malta, France, the United Kingdom, Switzerland, Canada and many other places. A member of the Association of Christian Therapists, she resides in Northern California. Visit her website at www.linda-schubert.com.

RICHARD DEMARCO is an international entrepreneur and promoter of contemporary arts. He is also an artist, gallery director and Professor of European Cultural Studies at Kingston University in the UK.

ROBERT FARICY is a member of the Jesuit order and Emeritus Professor of Spiritual Theology at the Pontifical Gregorian University in Rome, Italy. He is a noted speaker and the author of many books.

LIST OF ILLUSTRATIONS

(All projects in Malta)